SCHOLASTI

Beginning Cursive Practice

Copy & Write Quotes

Jane Lierman

NEW YORK • TORONTO • LONDON • AUCKLAND • SYDNEY
MEXICO CITY • NEW DELHI • HONG KONG • BUENOS AIRES

Teaching *Resources*

Dedicated to those who inspire others through their ideas, words, and actions.

Cover design by Maria Lilja
Interior design and illustrations by Robert Alemán Design
ISBN: 978-0-545-22754-4

1 2 3 4 5 6 7 8 9 10   40   18 17 16 15 14 13 12 11

Contents

Introduction

Beginning Cursive Practice: Copy & Write Quotes unites cursive practice with meaningful quotes for building character in your students. The cursive activity on each page provides practice for students who've mastered cursive letters, practiced letter combinations, and are ready to write words and short phrases. Each reproducible page contains an inspiring quote relating to a positive character trait such as kindness, honesty, or perseverance. The quotes can be used to generate discussion or to reinforce a class behavior goal. When all the cursive practice pages have been completed, each student can compile the pages into a mini-book keepsake of meaningful quotes.

Prerequisite Knowledge and Skills

Your students will have the most success with these lessons if they meet the following criteria:

- *Demonstrates correct pencil grip.*
- *Has mastered cursive letters.*
- *Has experience connecting letters, including those that connect to the next letter up high:* **b, o, v, w**

Daily Lesson: Five Simple Steps

To introduce the quotes and cursive practice, follow the steps below.
Important Note: Each reproducible page can be used for whole-group or individual practice. Whether students work independently or the entire lesson is completed as a group, it is important to complete Steps 1–3 together.

<table>
<tr><td>

STEP 1: Discuss the Quote and Character Trait

- Project the reproducible page onto a screen via an overhead projector, document camera, or SMART Board.
- Focus on the quote and read the quote to the students.
- Have the students read the quote with you.

</td><td>

</td></tr>
</table>

Materials
- Class set of a reproducible cursive practice quote page
- Class set of laminated alphabet and paper slant student reference cards (page 48)
- Pencils
- SMART Board, document camera, or overhead projector
- Optional: Class set of student dry erase lap boards

- Discuss the meaning of the quote and how it connects to students' lives.
- Discuss the picture in the middle of the page that symbolizes the quote's character trait.
- Give examples of times when you have seen the trait demonstrated in student behavior.
- Encourage students to generate examples.

STEP 2: Provide Cursive Instruction and Practice

- Keep the reproducible on the screen.
- Zoom in on the first key practice word at the top of each reproducible page.
- Read the key practice word while pointing to it, so students focus on the word.
- Discuss what they notice about how the letters connect.
- Model the correct letter strokes and connecting strokes for the first key word.
- Have students repeat your model in the air, on practice paper, or on lap boards.
- Remind students of any unusual letter connections. Pay particular attention to letter combinations that connect to the next letter at a high point: **b, o, v, w**. (See Teaching Tip #8.)
- Pass out the reproducible page and the laminated reference cards: Cursive alphabet with paper slant icons (page 48).
- Have students look at the right-hand or left-hand picture at the bottom of the cursive alphabet page and copy the turn. The turn depends on whether the student is right-handed or

left-handed. Check to see that each student has the appropriate alignment. (See Teaching Tip #4.)

- Remind students to follow the arrow direction when connecting letters.
- Have students trace the key word on the page.
- Allow time for students to practice the key word two times on the line and provide close supervision during these steps.
- Show and tell common errors you notice. Demonstrate and have students practice the correct format of common errors.

STEP 3: Continue Cursive Practice

- Zoom in on the next key practice word at the top of the reproducible page.
- Repeat process from **Step 2**.

STEP 4: Independent Practice

- Make sure students keep the cursive alphabet with directional arrows on their desks.
- Have students neatly write their name in cursive and add the date to the top of the page.
- Repeat the quote with them, pointing to the quote in the middle of the page.
- Encourage students to notice the capital and lowercase letter spacing within the lines.
- Have students neatly copy the quote on the lines at the bottom of the page.
- Review the key strokes and letter connections you worked on together.
- Remind students about:
  - Posture (See Teaching Tip #2.)
  - Pencil grip (See Teaching Tip #3.)
  - Paper alignment (See Teaching Tip #4.)
  - Proper spacing (finger width) between words. (See Teaching Tip #9.)
- Supervise students when they're writing, and have them fix errors and practice the correct format.

STEP 5 (OPTIONAL): Keepsake Quote Mini-Book

- Remind students they will save their cursive quote to create their own keepsake mini-book of character-building quotes.
- After students have received feedback and corrected errors, have them cut off the bottom section of the page along the dashed line by the scissor icon.
- Tell them to put their name or initials and the date on the back.
- Have students save the finished quotes in an envelope or file folder until all the quotes are completed.

MAKING A KEEPSAKE MINI-BOOK

If you plan to have students create a keepsake mini-book of these quotes, tell them that they will save each page to make a final mini-book. They will be able to take the book home, reread it for inspiration, and share it with friends and family for many years to come.

- Show students a finished spiral-bound version of the quote mini-book as a motivation to apply what they learn in each lesson.
- When students have corrected the final copy of a quote, have them follow the directions in **Daily Lesson: Step Five** to place the final quote in an envelope or file folder.
- At the end of the year, put the quotes in reverse order so the latest quote is first and the quote they completed first is at the end. Reverse order is an effective way to show student progress.
- For the front and back covers (approximately 4½ x 11 inches), have students decorate construction paper or use class art. Staple or spiral bind the pages and the covers.
  - Cover art ideas: marbled paper, water color, crayon resist.
  - Options: Add labels for byline and title; laminate covers for sturdiness.

Twelve Teaching Tips

Use these key cursive teaching tips for effective instruction and student practice. Teaching Tips are also referenced in the lesson steps.

1. **Provide close supervision**. Give immediate feedback. Have each student correct errors and practice correct format. It is difficult to unteach bad habits.

2. **Check posture**. Ensure that students are sitting up straight with both feet on the floor.

3. **Review pencil grip.** Review correct grips and why the right grip is critical to avoid hand and arm fatigue. Provide rubber pencil grips when necessary.

4. **Demonstrate slant**. Show students two cursive sample papers—one with a consistent slant and one with a mixed slant. Demonstrate how easy it is to achieve a consistent slant by keeping paper at a 45° angle. Remind them that there is a picture of the correct way to slant a paper for either a right-handed or a left-handed writer at the bottom of their cursive alphabet reference card.

   - Right-hander: lower left corner of paper points toward center of the body. Left hand holds the paper in place. Paper is at a 45° angle.
   - Left-hander: lower right corner of paper points toward center of the body. Right hand holds the paper in place. Paper is at a 45° angle.

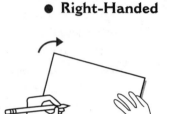

● **Right-Handed**

Left-Handed ●

5. **Remind students to follow arrow clues**. Take time to direct students' attention to the arrow clues on the practice words and on the cursive alphabet chart from page 48. Discuss letters that will connect to the next letter at the bottom and those that will connect at the top.

6. **Review letter and line alignment**.

   - All letters in a word must touch the bottom line.
   - Most lowercase letters touch the middle dotted line.
   - Lowercase letters **b**, **d**, **f**, **h**, **k**, **l**, **t** reach all the way to the top line.
   - Only lowercase letters **f**, **g**, **j**, **p**, **q**, **y** extend below the bottom line.
   - All uppercase letters touch the top line.
   - Only uppercase letters **J**, **Y**, **Z** extend below the bottom line.

7. **Remind students to close letters**. Remind students to make sure that closed letters are completely closed before they move on to the next letter.

8. **Explicitly teach letter combinations**. Teach the differences between these letter connections and review common errors.

   - Letters that finish at the top connect to the next letter up high: **b**, **o**, **v**, **w**.
   - All the other lowercase letters end low and connect to the next letter down low.

9. **Model correct spacing between words**. Use physical reminders such as finger width, small craft sticks, or the size of the letter o to help students recognize how much space is needed between words.

10. **Explain that letters are crossed and dotted after the entire word is written**. Teach students that letters are not crossed or dotted until the word is completely written, but that they must remember to cross or dot letters before moving on to the next word.

11. **Allow students to use a slant board**. Students who tire easily can use a slant board to increase endurance and speed. (Acrylic slant boards can be purchased through occupational therapists. You can make your own by attaching an empty tennis-ball can to the underside of clipboard. A binder will also work.)

12. **Modify length of assignment**. Lessons should be no longer than 10 or 15 minutes. If some students need shorter lessons, break the lessons into chunks and allow students to complete one part at a time.

Jumping for joy is good exercise.

—Author Unknown

Trace these words. Then practice writing them.

jumping

joy

Use your best cursive to copy the quote below.

✂

Attitude

Jumping for joy is good exercise.

Beginning Cursive Practice: Copy & Write Quotes © 2011 by Jane Lierman, Scholastic Teaching Resources

Name _____

Attitude is a little thing that makes a big difference.

—*Winston Churchill*

Trace these words. Then practice writing them.

Attitude

little

Use your best cursive to copy the quote below.

✂ -

Attitude

Attitude is a little thing that makes a big

difference.

Name _____

Date _____

The difference between "try" and "triumph" is a little "umph."

—Author Unknown

Trace these words. Then practice writing them.

between

try

Use your best cursive to copy the quote below.

✂ -

Attitude

The difference between "try" and "triumph" is a little "umph."

9

Beginning Cursive Practice: Copy & Write Quotes © 2011 by Jane Lierman, Scholastic Teaching Resources

Name _____

Date _____

A smile is a curve that sets things straight.

—P. Diller

Trace these words. Then practice writing them.

curve

straight

Use your best cursive to copy the quote below.

✂ -

Attitude

A smile is a curve that sets things

straight.

10

Name _____

The time is always right to do what is right.

—Martin Luther King, Jr.

Trace these words. Then practice writing them.

always

right

Use your best cursive to copy the quote below.

✂ -

Attitude

The time is always right to do what is

right.

Name _____

Date _____

Every minute you are angry, you lose 60 seconds of happiness.

—Ralph Waldo Emerson

Trace these words. Then practice writing them.

Every

angry

Use your best cursive to copy the quote below.

✂ -

Attitude

Every minute you are angry, you lose

60 seconds of happiness.

12

Name _____

Date _____

Good friends are worth more than jewels.

—*Author Unknown*

Trace these words. Then practice writing them.

friends

_____

jewels

_____

Use your best cursive to copy the quote below.

✂ -

Friendship

Good friends are worth more than

_____

jewels.

_____

Beginning Cursive Practice: Copy & Write Quotes © 2011 by Jane Lierman, Scholastic Teaching Resources

Name _____

Date _____

Hold a true friend with both your hands.

—*Nigerian Proverb*

Trace these words. Then practice writing them.

hold

_____

hands

_____

Use your best cursive to copy the quote below.

✂ -

Friendship

Hold a true friend with both your hands.

_____

_____

_____

Beginning Cursive Practice: Copy & Write Quotes © 2011 by Jane Lierman, Scholastic Teaching Resources

Friendship is a sheltering tree.

—Samuel Taylor Coleridge

Trace these words. Then practice writing them.

Friendship _____

sheltering _____

Use your best cursive to copy the quote below.

✂ -

Friendship

Friendship is a sheltering tree. _____

_____

_____

_____

Beginning Cursive Practice: Copy & Write Quotes © 2011 by Jane Lierman, Scholastic Teaching Resources

Name _____

Date _____

A friend's eye is a good mirror.

—Irish Proverb

Trace these words. Then practice writing them.

friend's

mirror

Use your best cursive to copy the quote below.

✄- -

Honesty

A friend's eye is a good mirror.

Name _____

Date _____

If you tell the truth, you don't have to remember anything.

—Mark Twain

Trace these words. Then practice writing them.

tell

don't

Use your best cursive to copy the quote below.

✂ -

Honesty

If you tell the truth, you don't have to

remember anything.

Name _____

Date _____

Half a truth is a whole lie.

—*Yiddish Proverb*

Trace these words. Then practice writing them.

half

whole

Use your best cursive to copy the quote below.

✂

Honesty

Half a truth is a whole lie.

Name _____

Date _____

Truth is a lifelong friend.

—Author Unknown

Trace these words. Then practice writing them.

Truth

lifelong

Use your best cursive to copy the quote below.

✂ --

Honesty

Truth is a lifelong friend.

19

Beginning Cursive Practice: Copy & Write Quotes © 2011 by Jane Lierman, Scholastic Teaching Resources

Name _____

Date _____

Do the right thing, even when no one is looking.

—Author Unknown

Trace these words. Then practice writing them.

right

looking

Use your best cursive to copy the quote below.

✂ -

Honesty

Do the right thing, even when no one is looking.

Name _____

Date _____

Kind words do not cost much, yet they accomplish much.

—Blaise Pascal

Trace these words. Then practice writing them.

Kind

accomplish

Use your best cursive to copy the quote below.

✂ - - - - - - - - - - - - - - - - - - -

Kindness

Kind words do not cost much, yet they accomplish much.

Beginning Cursive Practice: Copy & Write Quotes © 2011 by Jane Lierman, Scholastic Teaching Resources

Name _____

Date _____

Never lose a chance of saying a kind word.

—William Thackeray

Trace these words. Then practice writing them.

lose

word

Use your best cursive to copy the quote below.

✂

Kindness

Never lose a chance of saying a kind

word.

Name _____

Date _____

It's nice to be important, but it's important to always be nice.

—Alyssa Milano

Trace these words. Then practice writing them.

It's

important

Use your best cursive to copy the quote below.

✂ --

Kindness

It's nice to be important, but it's

important to always be nice.

23

Beginning Cursive Practice: Copy & Write Quotes © 2011 by Jane Lierman, Scholastic Teaching Resources

Name _____

Date _____

When you see a person without a smile, give him yours.

—Zig Ziglar

Trace these words. Then practice writing them.

person

smile

Use your best cursive to copy the quote below.

✂ -

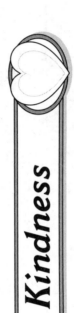

Kindness

When you see a person without a smile,

give him yours.

24

Name _____

Date _____

A book is a gift you can open again and again.

—Garrison Keillor

Trace these words. Then practice writing them.

gift

again

Use your best cursive to copy the quote below.

✂ -

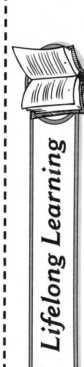

Lifelong Learning

A book is a gift you can open again and again.

Beginning Cursive Practice: Copy & Write Quotes © 2011 by Jane Lierman, Scholastic Teaching Resources

Reading gives us someplace to go when
we have to stay where we are.

—Mason Cooley

Trace these words. Then practice writing them.

when

where

Use your best cursive to copy the quote below.

✂

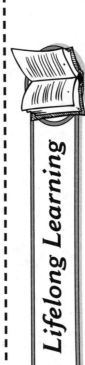

Lifelong Learning

Reading gives us someplace to go when

we have to stay where we are.

Name

Date

Not all readers are leaders, but all leaders are readers.

—Harry S. Truman

Trace these words. Then practice writing them.

readers

leaders

Use your best cursive to copy the quote below.

✂

Lifelong Learning

Not all readers are leaders, but all leaders are readers.

27

Name _____

Date _____

Your mind is like a parachute. It only works if it is open.

—Anthony D'Angelo

Trace these words. Then practice writing them.

parachute

works

Use your best cursive to copy the quote below.

✂ -

Lifelong Learning

Your mind is like a parachute. It only

works if it is open.

28

Name _____

Date _____

The more that you learn, the more places you'll go.

—Dr. Seuss

Trace these words. Then practice writing them.

more

you'll

Use your best cursive to copy the quote below.

✂ -

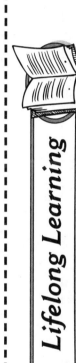

Lifelong Learning

The more that you learn, the more

places you'll go.

29

Name _____

Date _____

You learn something every day if you pay attention.

—Ray LeBlond

Trace these words. Then practice writing them.

you

pay

Use your best cursive to copy the quote below.

✂

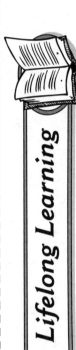

Lifelong Learning

You learn something every day if you pay attention.

Name _____

Date _____

Stand up for what is right, even if you're standing alone.

—Author Unknown

Trace these words. Then practice writing them.

right

you're

Use your best cursive to copy the quote below.

✂ --

Making a Difference

Stand up for what is right, even if

you're standing alone.

Beginning Cursive Practice: Copy & Write Quotes © 2011 by Jane Lierman, Scholastic Teaching Resources

Take care of the Earth, and she will take care of you.

—Author Unknown

Trace these words. Then practice writing them.

Take

Earth

Use your best cursive to copy the quote below.

✂

Making a Difference

Take care of the Earth, and she will take

care of you.

Actions speak louder than words.

—Proverb

Trace these words. Then practice writing them.

Actions

_____

speak

_____

Use your best cursive to copy the quote below.

✂ -

Making a Difference

Actions speak louder than words.

_____

_____

_____

Beginning Cursive Practice: Copy & Write Quotes © 2011 by Jane Lierman, Scholastic Teaching Resources

You never know what you can do until you try.

—Author Unknown

Trace these words. Then practice writing them.

never _____

know _____

Use your best cursive to copy the quote below.

✂ -

Perseverance

You never know what you can do

until you try.

It takes both rain and sunshine to make a rainbow.

—*Author Unknown*

Trace these words. Then practice writing them.

sunshine

rainbow

Use your best cursive to copy the quote below.

Perseverance

It takes both rain and sunshine to

make a rainbow.

Name _____

Date _____

You never really lose until you quit trying.

—Mike Ditka

Trace these words. Then practice writing them.

until

quit

Use your best cursive to copy the quote below.

✂ -

Perseverance

You never really lose until you quit trying.

36

Name _____

Date _____

Winners never quit, and quitters never win.

—*Vince Lombardi*

Trace these words. Then practice writing them.

Winners

quitters

Use your best cursive to copy the quote below.

✂ -

Perseverance

Winners never quit, and quitters never

win.

Beginning Cursive Practice: Copy & Write Quotes © 2011 by Jane Lierman, Scholastic Teaching Resources

If at first you don't succeed, try, try again.

—Thomas Palmer

Trace these words. Then practice writing them.

first

succeed

Use your best cursive to copy the quote below.

✂

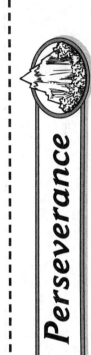

Perseverance

If at first you don't succeed, try, try

again.

Beginning Cursive Practice: Copy & Write Quotes © 2011 by Jane Lierman, Scholastic Teaching Resources

Name _____

Date _____

Improvement begins with " I ."

—Arnold H. Glasgow

Trace these words. Then practice writing them.

Improvement

I

Use your best cursive to copy the quote below.

✂ -

Perseverance

Improvement begins with " I ."

39

Name _____

Date _____

Don't think "problem," think "opportunity."

—Author Unknown

Trace these words. Then practice writing them.

problem

_____

opportunity

_____

Use your best cursive to copy the quote below.

✂ -

Perseverance

Don't think "problem," think

_____

"opportunity."

_____

40

Beginning Cursive Practice: Copy & Write Quotes © 2011 by Jane Lierman, Scholastic Teaching Resources

Name _____

Never, never, never give up.

—*Winston Churchill*

Trace these words. Then practice writing them.

give

up

Use your best cursive to copy the quote below.

✂ -

Perseverance

Never, never, never give up.

Beginning Cursive Practice: Copy & Write Quotes © 2011 by Jane Lierman, Scholastic Teaching Resources

Name _____

Date _____

Look for your choices, pick the best one, and then go for it.

—Pat Riley

Trace these words. Then practice writing them.

Look

for

Use your best cursive to copy the quote below.

✄

Perseverance

Look for your choices, pick the best one,

and then go for it.

42

Name ______________________ Date ______________________

Nothing will work unless you do.

—*Maya Angelou*

Trace these words. Then practice writing them.

Nothing

unless

Use your best cursive to copy the quote below.

Perseverance

Nothing will work unless you do.

Beginning Cursive Practice: Copy & Write Quotes © 2011 by Jane Lierman, Scholastic Teaching Resources

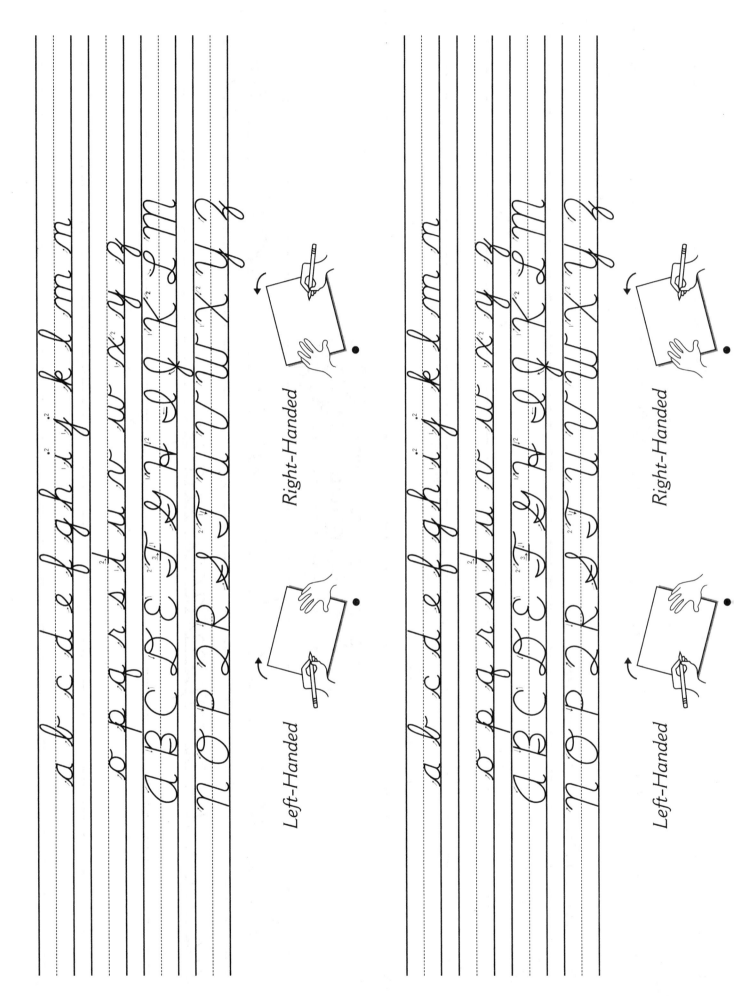

Right-Handed

Left-Handed

Right-Handed

Left-Handed

48